My Grandpa A to Z

Fill In The Blank Gift Book

Printed in USA

Published by K. Francklin

Cover Image: Produced by K. Francklin

© Copyright 2015

ISBN-13: 978-1517754532

ISBN-10: 1517754534

I Love My Grandpa Because…

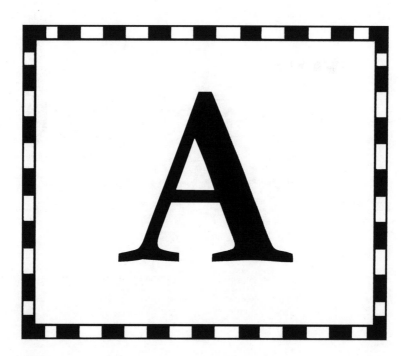

My Grandpa is...

A_____

B

My Grandpa is…

B_____

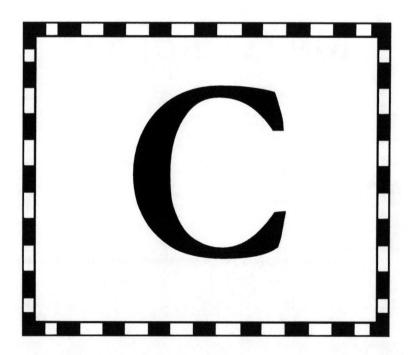

My Grandpa is...

C_____

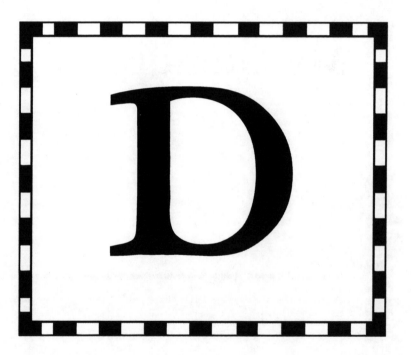

My Grandpa is...

D_____

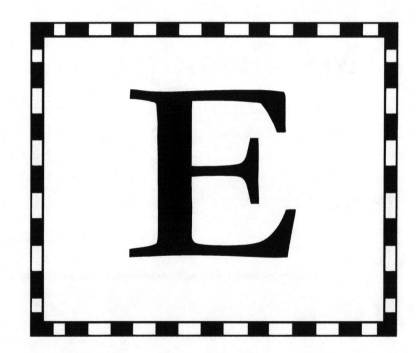

My Grandpa is...

E_____

My Grandpa is…

F_____

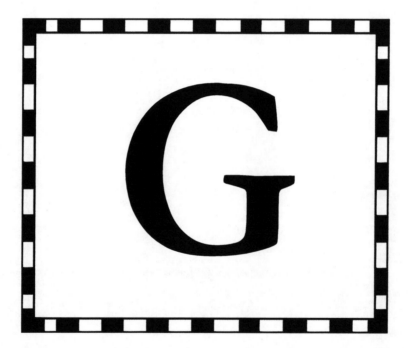

My Grandpa is...

G_____

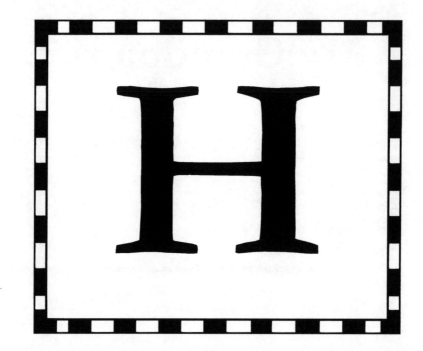

My Grandpa is...

H_____

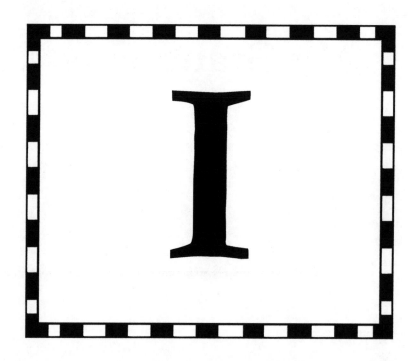

My Grandpa is...

I_____

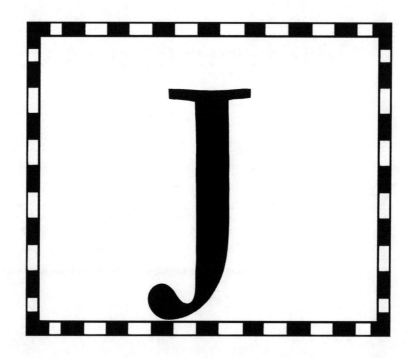

My Grandpa is…

J_____

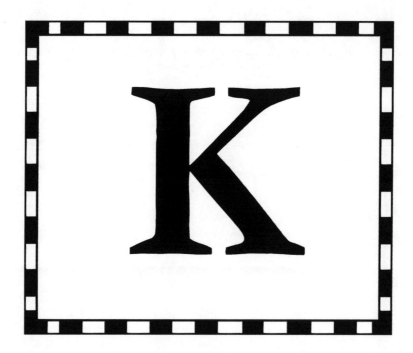

My Grandpa is…

K_____

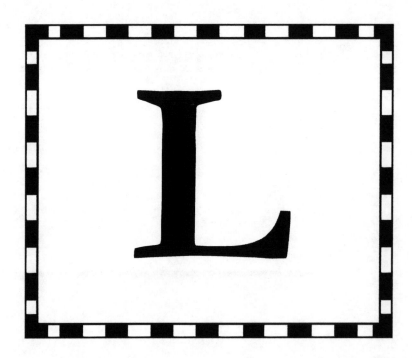

My Grandpa is…

L_____

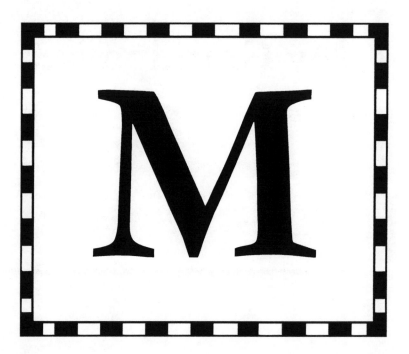

My Grandpa is...

M_____

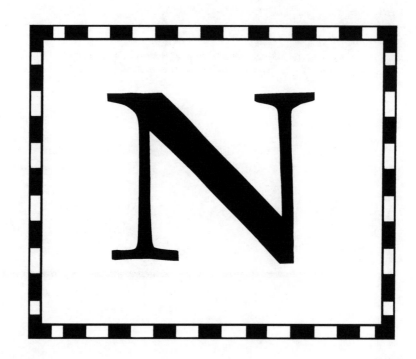

My Grandpa is...

N_____

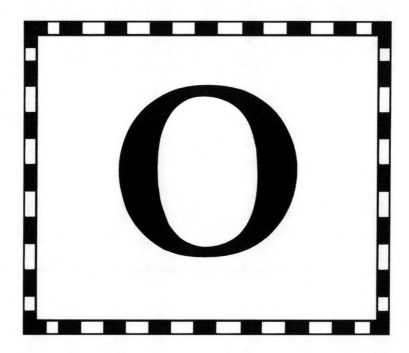

My Grandpa is...

O_____

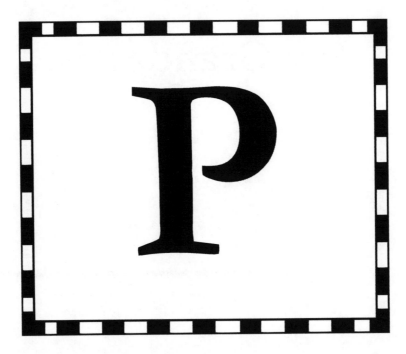

My Grandpa is…

P _____

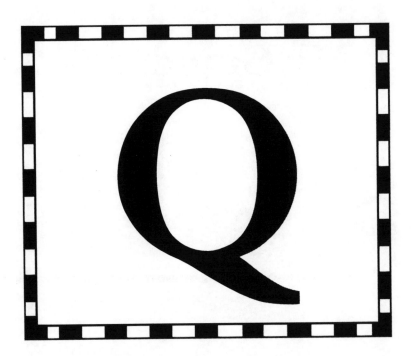

My Grandpa is...

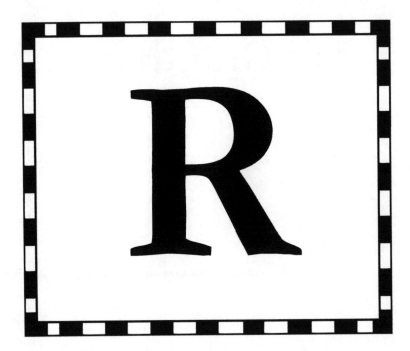

My Grandpa is…

R_____

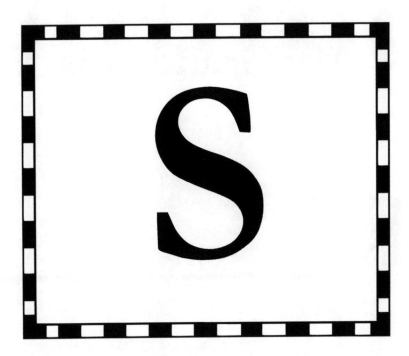

My Grandpa is...

S _____

My Grandpa is...

T_____

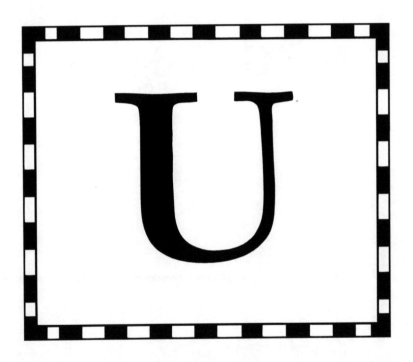

My Grandpa is...

U_____

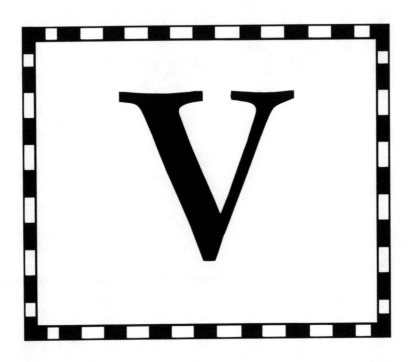

My Grandpa is...

V_____

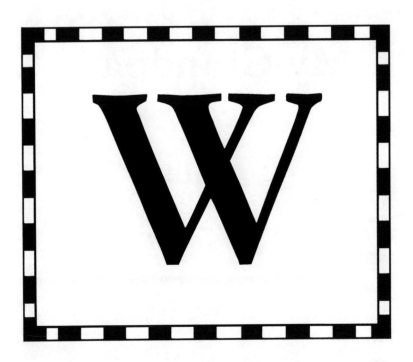

My Grandpa is...

W_____

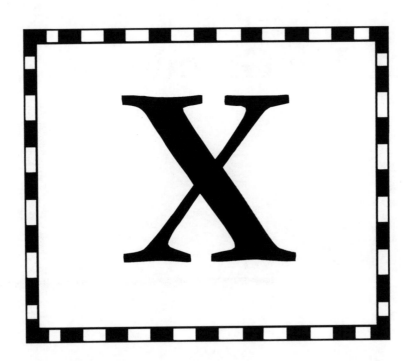

My Grandpa is…

X<u>   </u>

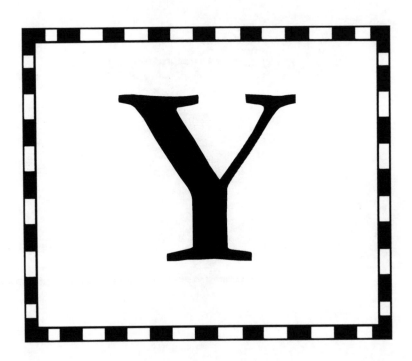

My Grandpa is...

Y_____

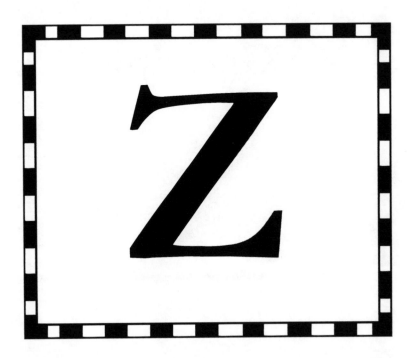

My Grandpa is...

Z_____

Thank You!

Also In This Series

My Dad/Papa A to Z

My Mom/Mum/Mama A to Z

My Son A to Z

My Daughter A to Z

My Husband A to Z

My Wife A to Z

My Sister A to Z

My Brother A to Z

My Grandpa/Grandad/Gramps A to Z

My Grandma/Granny/Nanny/Gran/Nana A to Z

My Best Friend/Bestie A to Z

My Girlfriend A to Z

My Boyfriend A to Z

My Partner A to Z

Made in the USA
Lexington, KY
22 January 2017